The Collingwoods

A Brief History of The Ancient Northumberland Family

S.P. Collingwood-Jones

Published in 2022
by S.P. Collingwood-Jones

© S.P. Collingwood-Jones 2022
collingwoodbook@gmail.com

ISBN: 978-1-913898-32-8

Book Production by Russell Holden
www.pixeltweakspublications.com

All rights reserved without limiting the rights under copyright reserved above, no parts of this publication may be reproduced, stored in or introduced into a retrieval system, or transmitted in any form, or by any means (electronic, mechanical, photocopying, recording or otherwise) without the prior written permission of both the copyright owner and the publisher of this book.

Images sourced under the Creative Commons usage rights are indicated with the CC icon ⓒ

Permission to use the image on P.60 kindly given by Chris Collingwood. Reproduction of this image without consent is strictly forbidden.

I dedicate this book...

To my Nan Collingwood as without her stories I might never have looked into the Collingwood branch of my family and not known of their involvement in this country's history...

To my wife who helped with the research...

To my children and grandchildren, (the latest descendants), who I hope will find the past history of this branch of their family as interesting as I do.

Nan

Contents

Introduction 1

Chapter 1   The Collingwoods 5

Chapter 2   Admiral Lord Collingwood 9

Chapter 3   Individual Collingwoods 20

Chapter 4   The Border Reivers 28

Chapter 5   The Pele Towers 33

Chapter 6   The Jacobites 35

Chapter 7   Collingwood Settlers 37

Chapter 8   The Connected Families 39

Chapter 9   Further Back in Time 51

Chapter 10 Famous Collingwoods 54

Chapter 11 Miscellaneous 61

Flag of Northumberland

Map of some of the places mentioned in the book

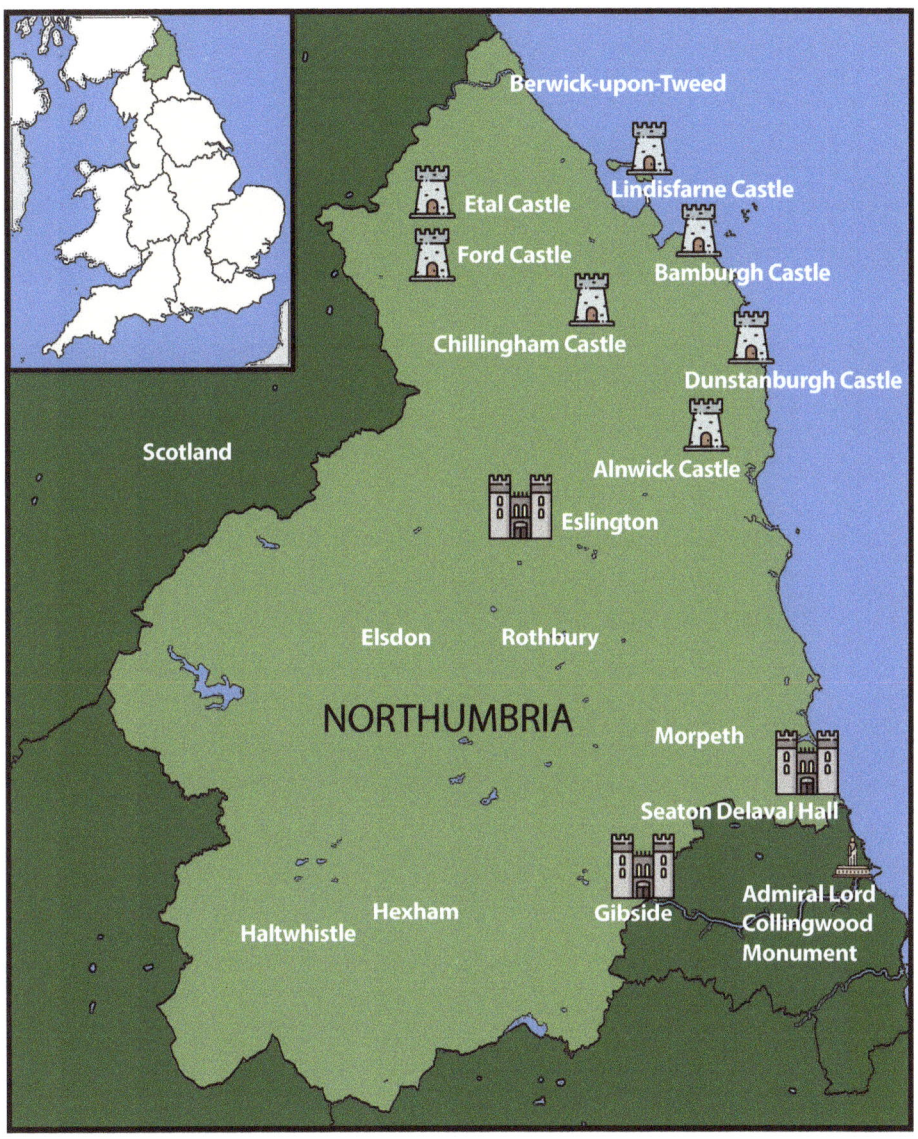

Introduction

When I was young my Nan Collingwood always used to tell us stories of how there were lords and ladies in the family years ago. This was taken with a pinch of salt for most of the time but it was always my intention to trace the family tree when I had the time, particularly to see if I was in any way related to Admiral Lord Collingwood. And so when the Coronavirus arrived and with it lockdown, the time had finally come to start my research.

I knew a bit of the history of my Nan's family going back a couple of generations, but have now discovered that it was my great grandfather x2 that left Northumberland in the 1800's and headed to London, presumably for work. However, nothing could have prepared me for what I have since discovered with regard to the Collingwood family, the amount of history connected with the family seems to be never-ending and I have discovered that I and a lot of the other Collingwood descendants are also related to royalty and a Viking. The most famous Collingwood I have discovered so far is, of course, Admiral Lord Collingwood of Trafalgar fame.

When I was doing my research many various links from different aspects of history such as the Battle of Naseby, the Border Reivers and the Jacobite Rebellion to name but a few came to light, all connected by one thing, Collingwoods! Part of the idea of this book is to consolidate in to one place the information I have discovered so far, and to give a little insight as to what life was like for some Collingwoods.

I am going to detail some individual family members and the information I have about them, some just a snippet and others, such as Admiral Lord Collingwood, there is a lot of information and history. Whilst I cannot cover all the Collingwoods, I am hoping to give a snapshot of life over the years, and give pointers for people who are doing further research of their own.

You will see in the book that as well as giving a name I also give the year of birth. This is purely for the reason of identifying individuals as the same names were used over and over again down the years. Additionally, where I mention a link between the Collingwoods and other families by marriage, it is quite often the case that over the years more than one member of the linked families married into the Collingwoods but there is not enough space in this book for me to list everyone.

I will be detailing some of the more interesting members of the Collingwood family that I have discovered so far, starting with the more recent and then working my way back through the years, and the family certainly goes back a great many! It is said that the Collingwoods were a very ancient Northumberland family and it is likely that the name may even have originated in Northumberland.

Introduction

At times there is a slight variation in the spelling of Collingwood but that is to be expected considering the dates we are looking at, (this is also the case for some of the other surnames and place names connected with the Collingwoods). The dates I detail in this book are correct to the best of my knowledge from the research I have done.

I have discovered that there are many branches of the Collingwood family, now spread all around the world, but many of these branches can in fact probably trace their ancestors back to the 1500's or an earlier date, as indeed I have. With the Collingwood family being who they were there is quite a lot written about them in various places and there is plenty of information available on the internet. Some of the information I have given in this book is from that which is free to access on the internet.

I for one, never realised just how much fighting there was in the border lands between Scotland and England over the years, how much the actual border moved back and forth and just how brutal life was in those times, and it seems the Collingwood family were involved a lot of the time. It is also interesting to note that when we look at the other large landowning families that married into the Collingwoods or vice versa, between them they would have owned a very large area of Northumberland in the 1400's and 1500's.

Further on in this book I give a little information about some of the families that became linked to the Collingwoods through marriage as again there is a tremendous amount of history involved with most of them.

I hope readers of this book will find it interesting and that it will prove useful to those who are tracing their Collingwood family tree.

CHAPTER ONE

THE COLLINGWOODS

The family seat of my line of the Collingwoods for many years was Eslington Park near Rothbury in Northumberland. Eslington was first mentioned in the reign of King Edward III and was held in early times by a family of that name. It later passed into the hands of the Hazelriggs, the Herons and then to the Collingwoods.

As to where the Collingwood name originates, the most popular theory being that it derived from the village of Coanwood and translates as "hazel woods". Coanwood village is in the Parish of Haltwhistle in Northumberland. It is known for coal mining, (1860's-1930), and did have a railway station until it was closed in 1976. In the past the village would have been a busier place than it is today. There are also a lot of theories as to who was the first Collingwood but as nothing can be proven for definite we shall probably never know for certain, possibly a farmer who lived in Coanwood or possibly a farmer who had hazel trees?

A lot of the branches of the Collingwoods that I have investigated lead back to Sir Cuthbert Collingwood 1538. I am lucky in that with the history attached to my particular line of the family it is very well documented which makes it a lot easier to trace. However, for some of the other branches it is not so easy and unless a link can be found between the more recent descendants and the past they are unable to get back as far as I have.

Going back to Cuthbert 1538, it is evident that the Collingwood family had been a significant force in Northumberland even before his time. In the 13th century a number of the Northumberland families had developed important standings on the English side of the border. The Collingwoods, along with other families such as the Greys, Herons, Lilburns, Percys and Selbys. Some of the families were more feared than others, the Percy family being one such family.

Reiving was mostly about the theft of property and livestock while actual exchange of land ownership was mostly by gift or purchase, such as an inheritance or marriage.

These families fought the Scots but they also fought with each other, and during these fights livestock would be stolen and they would often pillage their rival's settlements. Some of the raiding would not be confined to small reiving bands but could involve hundreds of men. In 1587 it is said that Cuthbert Collingwood 1538 took nearly 900 men on a raid into Teviotdale and in reprisal Lord Cessford from the Scots side brought two or three thousand men, some on foot, some mounted, to raid the Eslington land.

These families erected Pele towers on their lands, both to show their power and for defensive purposes. These towers could be found widely in Northumberland. The bigger landowners would construct these towers out of stone, but less influential families would use wood.

The reiving period largely ended with the Act of Union in 1603, after which there was much more control in the Border areas. At this time the Collingwoods also held part of Whittingham which they had purchased from the Heron family earlier in the century. Glanton at this time was roughly divided in half between the Collingwoods of Eslington and the Proctors of Shawdon.

At the time of the English Civil Wars in the mid 1600's the question of religion and loyalty to the Crown and Parliament became very important. The Collingwoods of Eslington were Roman Catholic and royalist.

In 1644 Eslington was forfeited to Parliamentary ownership but in 1656 the Collingwoods were able to buy back their estate, although in the meantime Sir Arthur Hazelrigg had managed to get legal possession of Eslington and demanded rent from the Collingwoods, which they would not pay. After seven years of legal action and the restoration of the monarchy the dispute was settled in favour of the Collingwoods.

Unfortunately no lesson seems to have been learned from this event as in the early 1700's the Collingwoods showed support for the Stuarts during this period of the Jacobite rebellions and once again had their Eslington estate taken from them. I give more details about this in the section about William Collingwood 1655 in the Individual Collingwoods chapter.

Some of the places in Northumberland that were strongly associated with the Collingwoods in the past were Brandon, Chirton, Dalden, Dissington, Eglingham, Eslington, Etal, Glanton, Lilburn, Little Ryle and Stanhope.

The Collingwood motto:

Nil conscire sibi

translates as

To have a conscience free from guilt.

Etal Castle

CHAPTER TWO

ADMIRAL LORD COLLINGWOOD
1748 – 1810

After all the years I spent wondering if I was related to Admiral Lord Cuthbert Collingwood, it turns out he is a 5th cousin. Cuthbert Collingwood is one of the most famous members of the Collingwood family, if not the most famous. Cuthbert was born in 1748 to his parents Cuthbert Collingwood 1712 and Milcah Dobson.

I will only give a brief synopsis of Cuthbert in this book, as there is so much history connected to him that it would need a whole book just to detail his life and indeed there are numerous books already written about Cuthbert readily available. However, given Cuthbert's place in history I would like to detail in this book just a few of his major achievements.

Admiral Lord Cuthbert Collingwood is known by various names, 'The Unsung Hero', 'Northumberland's Heart of Oak', 'The Northumbrian Who Saved the Nation' being a few of them. Cuthbert was born in Newcastle-upon-Tyne and attended the city's grammar school until the age of eleven when he joined the Royal Navy. He fought in many battles and worked his way up through the ranks, along with his friend Horatio Nelson.

Cuthbert married Sarah Blackett and they had two daughters, Mary Patience 1773 and Sarah 1792. However, due to his naval duties Cuthbert was rarely at home. Sarah Blackett was a granddaughter of Admiral Roddam. Cuthbert and Sarah had a house in Morpeth, Collingwood House, which is still there today, and at the time of writing this book it is usually open to the public annually on the Heritage weekends in September. When he was at home in Morpeth, Cuthbert liked to visit Newbiggin-by-the-Sea and would take his daughters there, and there is now a Collingwood Road in Newbiggin-by-the-sea.

The most famous battle that Cuthbert fought in was Trafalgar, and this is where the unsung hero comes into play as many felt that Cuthbert did not get enough recognition for his part in the battle. Now I have researched this I can see how this comes about. It turns out that Cuthbert's ship, HMS *Royal Sovereign*, got to the battle lines first and fired the first shots. HMS *Royal Sovereign* had just had a new copper bottom and this made her the fastest ship of the fleet.

At Trafalgar when the enemy opened fire, it was the Blue Ensign that Cuthbert hoisted, signalling his status as Vice-Admiral of the Blue.

Nelson was shot by a French sniper between the hours of 1pm and 2pm and it was at this time that Cuthbert took overall command on 21st October 1805. Earlier in the day Cuthbert had engaged no fewer than five of the enemy fleet, disabling the mighty *Santa Anna* with a point-blank broadside salvo before the rest of the British Navy could catch up. At the same time four other ships were attacking Cuthbert's ship from all quarters. However, Cuthbert manoeuvred in such a way that much of the enemy fire ended up falling as friendly fire upon its own craft. This act prompted Nelson to say, just hours before he was fatally wounded, "see how that noble fellow Collingwood takes his ship into action, how I envy him". After Nelson was wounded Cuthbert took overall command of the fleet, carried on fighting and won the battle. Cuthbert did sustain some injuries to his leg from splinters that flew around following a cannonball strike.

The winning of this battle ultimately secured Britain's dominance of the seas and paved the way for Wellington's victory of Napoleon at Waterloo ten years later. Cuthbert also managed to get all the fleet safely back to harbour with no losses even though there was a very bad storm raging.

The timings of the Battle of Trafalgar

The preparation for the battle began at 6 a.m. on the 21st October 1805. The British and French/Spanish fleets sighted each other at 6.40 a.m. but due to very little wind it took until 11.45 a.m. to get close enough to engage the enemy. Nelson gave the order to prepare for battle. The French/Spanish fleet was sailing in a line off Cape Trafalgar. The British came up from the west forming two parallel lines.

Cuthbert gathered his officers to give one last inspirational message - "now gentlemen let us do something today which the world may talk of hereafter".

The British fleet was out-numbered, the enemy totalled nearly 30,000 men and 2,632 guns to the British 18,000 men and 2,148 guns. At 11.45 a.m. Nelson ordered the famous signal from The *Victory*, "England expects every man to do his duty". At 11.50 a.m. the French

Commander, Pierre Charles Jean Baptiste Sivestre de Villeneuve, sent a signal to engage the British ships.

Cuthbert was the first to reach the enemy line, firing a broadside into the *Santa Anna* and slicing the French/Spanish fleet in two. The *Santa Anna* struck her colours, (surrendered) at 2.20 p.m. Cuthbert took command after hearing that Nelson had been shot and led the British fleet to victory, the battle ceasing at 5.30 p.m.

Seventeen enemy ships had been captured, one was ablaze, eleven struggled back to Cadiz but were captured later. A total of 449 British sailors were killed and 1,217 wounded. The enemy's losses were much worse with 4,408 dead, 2,545 wounded and 20,000 taken prisoner.

Cuthbert was well known for the frequent drilling of his gunnery crew. Cuthbert believed that if a ship could release three well aimed broadsides in five minutes "no enemy could resist them".

For his services he was created Baron Collingwood and granted a pension of £2,000 a year. Cuthbert was also awarded three naval gold medals for his part in the Glorious 1st of June, Cape Vincent and Trafalgar battles. Only Nelson and Sir Edmund Bury have also been awarded the same amount.

Cuthbert was also presented with a ceremonial sword and scabbard by the City of London. This award is only given to military men and the value at that time was 100-200 guineas. Only 63 such swords have ever been presented, the last two awards were for the Falklands War in 1982. The Admiral of the *Santa Anna* also presented his sword to Cuthbert as a mark of surrender. Cuthbert was also presented with a further sword from the Admiralty for his part in the Battle of Trafalgar.

Another interesting feat that Cuthbert achieved was after he was appointed to command a squadron and had orders to pursue the French fleet which had sailed from Toulon. The combined fleets of Spain and France were returning to Cadiz and on their way they encountered Cuthbert's

The British Fleet

COLLINGWOOD COMMAND	NELSON COMMAND
HMS *Royal Sovereign*	HMS *Victory*
HMS *Achille*	HMS *Africa*
HMS *Belleisle*	HMS *Agamemnon*
HMS *Bellerophon*	HMS *Ajax*
HMS *Collossus*	HMS *Britannia*
HMS *Defence*	HMS *Conqueror*
HMS *Defiance*	HMS *Entreprenant* *
HMS *Dreadnought*	HMS *Euryalus* *
HMS *Mars*	HMS *Leviathan*
HMS *Polyphemus*	HMS *Minotaur*
HMS *Prince*	HMS *Naiad* *
HMS *Revenge*	HMS *Neptune*
HMS *Swiftsure*	HMS *Orion*
HMS *Thunderer*	HMS *Phobe* *
HMS *Tonnant*	HMS *Pickle* *
	HMS *Sirius* *
	HMS *Spartiate*
	HMS *Téméraire*

* frigates

fleet off Cadiz, which only consisted of four ships including his own. Cuthbert managed to avoid the pursuit although he was chased by sixteen enemy ships. Before half of the enemy's fleet had entered the harbour he had resumed the blockade and used false signals to disguise the size of his squadron.

Later in his life Cuthbert suffered with ill health, and although repeatedly asking to be allowed to come home the Admiralty did not permit this. This is very sad considering the service he had given throughout his career.

Cuthbert spent five years on Menorca and during his time there he purchased a house. Today the house is a hotel, Hotel Del Almirante. The Manager gives a talk once a week about the Admiral to the guests. Looking at photos of the hotel online, I can see that many of the rooms have lots of pictures featuring various ships. The hotel has a collection of heirlooms relating to Admiral Lord Collingwood's time. Hopefully once the Coronavirus has moved on I will have an opportunity to visit the hotel.

The Collingwood Society, based in Trinity House, Newcastle-upon-Tyne just some 400 meters from where Admiral Lord Collingwood was born, is a special interest group focusing on the life, times and legacy of Admiral Lord Collingwood. Although the society is based in the north east of England it has a worldwide membership.

Trafalgar Day is celebrated every year on the 21st October, and whilst in many places Nelson is celebrated, in Tyneside and Morpeth the toast is to Admiral Lord Collingwood. The Admiral is regarded as a local hero and a national hero.

ADMIRAL LORD COLLINGWOOD 1748 – 1810

A monument was built in Tynemouth in 1845 and is a symbol of the pride that has been inspired by Admiral Lord Collingwood's naval skills, leadership and compassion which inspired all the men under his command. Current plans are afoot to illuminate the monument so that all those who enter the Tyne of an evening will see Admiral Lord Collingwood standing tall. The four 32lb cannon that are placed on the monument are from HMS *Royal Sovereign*. The monument is grade II listed.

There are also other busts and portraits of Admiral Lord Collingwood in various locations around the country. Collingwood's achievements were recognised in a career that saw him promoted ultimately to the status of Admiral.

Looking into all the information about Admiral Lord Collingwood it is revealed that he was an intensely loyal and reticent man who put duty to country before all else. Cuthbert was known by many of his crews as "father". Cuthbert detested flogging and brutality.

Admiral Lord Collingwood Monument in Tynemouth

After the Battle of Trafalgar Cuthbert spent his remaining years in charge of the Mediterranean fleet, scarcely setting foot in Britain and hardly seeing his family. In fact he did not spend much time on land at all, his time was mainly spent aboard ship. After Trafalgar there was not the need for much fighting at sea, just the bureaucracy of running a fleet to maintain a stranglehold on the Mediterranean. Cuthbert found this boring and immensely time consuming. His working day would usually be something like 5 a.m. to about midnight.

Cuthbert was considered to be irreplaceable by the King and ministers and so effectively was worked to death despite his pleas to return home on health grounds. Another issue was that the Duke of Clarence, (the future William IV), had put in for the Mediterranean job thus giving the Admiralty a dilemma. Should they offend the Duke by rejecting his application or appoint him even though they knew he would be incompetent at the job. The solution they came up with was to keep Cuthbert in his position, despite his pleas to be allowed to come home. Cuthbert was also regarded by the Admiralty as a good diplomat, and this was another reason to keep him overseas. Eventually on the 3rd March 1810 Cuthbert was given permission to come home but he died on the 7th March 1810 whilst on the voyage home. During the 50 years Cuthbert was in the Senior Service 45 of these were spent away from home.

Cuthbert's faithful dog was Bounce and he was aboard ship with Cuthbert, unfortunately falling overboard one night, not long before the time of Cuthbert's own death.

Cuthbert's first action was at Bunker Hill in 1775, a North American battle during the siege of Boston that aided his promotion to Lieutenant. It was in the West Indies after this that he began his thirty year friendship with Horatio Nelson. Nelson was ten years his junior but always just senior in rank to Cuthbert. In fact after 1779 Cuthbert and Nelson rose through the ranks with Cuthbert always being one rank below Nelson right up to the time of Trafalgar. Nelson's nickname for Cuthbert was "Coll".

In 1806 Cuthbert inherited Chirton Hall by the Tyne from his cousin Edward Collingwood of Dissington but he never lived there.

Another thing that Cuthbert was famous for was for planting acorns when he went walking in the Northumberland countryside so that there would be an ample supply of oak to be used for ship building in the future.

Captain Wilfred Collingwood was one of Cuthbert's younger brothers, and occasionally they served in the same conflicts. Wilfred also served with Nelson. Wilfred died at sea on the 21st April 1787 from tuberculosis, and was buried in a military ceremony on St Vincent's.

Cuthbert's tomb is in St Paul's cathedral next to his friend Nelson.

SHIPS THAT CUTHBERT SERVED ON

SHIP	RANK	ACTION
HMS *Shannon*	Able Seaman 1761-65	
HMS *Gibraltar*	Midshipman 1776-67	
HMS *Liverpool*	Master's Mate 1767-72	
HMS *Lennox*	Midshipman 1773 Master's Mate 1773 Midshipman 1774	
HMS *Preston*	Midshipman Master's Mate 1774-75	Bunker Hill 17.6.1775
HMS *Somerset*	4th Lieutenant 1775-76	
HMS *Hornet*	Lieutenant 1776-78	
HMS *Lowestoffe*	2nd Lieutenant 1778	
HMS *Badger*	Commander 1779-80	
HMS *Hinchingbrooke*	Captain 1780	
HMS *Pelican*	Commander 1780-81	Shipwrecked in a hurricane
HMS *Sampson*	Captain 1783	
HMS *Mediator*	Captain 1783	West Indies
HMS *Mermaid*	Captain 1790-91	
HMS *Prince*	Captain 1793-94	
HMS *Hector*	Captain 1794	
HMS *Excellent*	Captain 1774-99	Battle of Cape St Vincent 1797
HMS *Triumph*	Rear Admiral of the White	
HMS *Barfleur*	Rear Admiral of the White 1800-02	Glorious 1st of June
HMS *Diamond*	Rear Admiral of the Red 1803	
HMS *Venerable*	Rear Admiral of the Red 1803	

ADMIRAL LORD COLLINGWOOD 1748 – 1810

SHIP	RANK	ACTION
HMS *Minotaur*	1803	
HMS *Venerable*	1803	
HMS *Colossus*	1803-04	
HMS *Culloden*	Rear Admiral of the Red 1803 Vice Admiral of the Blue 1804	
HMS *Prince*	Vice Admiral of the Blue 1804	
HMS *Dreadnought*	Vice Admiral of the Blue 1804-05	
HMS *Royal Sovereign*	Vice Admiral of the Blue 1805	Trafalgar
HMS *Euryalus*	Vice Admiral of the Blue 1805	Peacekeeping in the Mediterranean
HMS *Queen*	Vice Admiral of the Red 1805-06	Peacekeeping in the Mediterranean
HMS *Ocean*	Vice Admiral of the Red 1806-09	Peacekeeping in the Mediterranean
HMS *Ville De Paris*	1809-10	Peacekeeping in the Mediterranean

Many things have been named after Admiral Lord Collingwood over the years in recognition of his services.

- The naval base in Fareham, Hampshire and several ships
- A few towns in various countries around the world, many streets, pubs and buildings, including a school house at the Royal Grammar school in Newcastle.
- Admiral Collingwood Cheese and Admiral Collingwood Gin. Collingwood paint, which is a warm gray paint colour.
- 1978-1992 British Rail locomotive 50005 was named Collingwood and in 2005 locomotive 90020 was named Collingwood at Newcastle station.
- It is also rumoured that the film Master and Commander was based on some of the exploits of Cuthbert.

CHAPTER THREE

INDIVIDUAL COLLINGWOODS

WILLIAM COLLINGWOOD 1655 & GEORGE COLLINGWOOD 1653

William is my great grandfather x 8 and the reason he gets a mention is that his brother George 1653 decided to fight on the side of the Jacobites at the first rebellion in 1715.

Unfortunately George was captured at the Battle of Preston and was hung, drawn and quartered in Liverpool in 1716. It seems that George was somewhat unfortunate as the captured prisoners were supposed to be taken to London to be tried but George took ill with gout when they were at Wigan and so was tried in Liverpool instead. The other prisoners were taken to London where the trials continued but not all were executed. If George had made it to London his fate might have been different.

Another subsequent and very unfortunate consequence of George getting caught was that the Crown seized the family seat of Eslington Park and all the lands that they owned.

Sir Henry Liddell of Ravensworth Castle paid the Crown the sum of £18,100 for the Eslington estate in 1720. The original house is now no longer standing but a newer house was built on the site in 1720 by the new owner, which was extended in 1796. A lot of the estate has been sold off over the years because of death duties. The current house is now Grade II listed. Lord Ravensworth, (Thomas Liddell), now lives at Eslington Park. The Liddell family is distantly related to the Collingwoods.

The Collingwoods had had a long line of family members who served as High Sheriffs of Northumberland but the execution of George 1653 put a stop to this. Many Royalists fled for fear of retribution and loss of lands and many relatives with the surname of Collingwood left the Northumberland area and travelled to London and other cities. Some changed their surname to something other than Collingwood. It took the Collingwoods time to recover from the stigma of George 1653.

GEORGE COLLINGWOOD 1629 & BENEDICT 1622

The next person of interest is my great grandfather x9, and again it is a brother of George 1629 that is of interest. Benedict 1622 fought and was killed at The Battle of Naseby.

SIR GEORGE COLLINGWOOD 1571

As you can see from my next great grandfather we start to get to the titled family members, and I presume this is where my Nan's stories came from, and they were stories that were obviously passed down through the generations. Understandably with the family having owned a family seat and lands which they lost, there was no doubt considerable upset which was talked about and passed down through each subsequent generation.

Sir George 1571 is my great grandfather x11. The reason this George gets a mention is again due to his brother Cuthbert Collingwood 1567. It is this Cuthbert's line that goes on to Admiral Lord Collingwood.

SIR CUTHBERT COLLINGWOOD 1538

Sir Cuthbert 1538 is my great grandfather x12, and he married Lady Dorothy Bowes. Sir Cuthbert 1538 is the son of Sir John Collingwood 1512 and Ursula Buckton. Sir John was High Sheriff of Northumberland.

Sir Cuthbert 1538 was High Sheriff of Northumberland and lived at Eslington Park. From the documented history that I have seen I imagine Sir Cuthbert led an interesting life, albeit dangerous at times, and I detail a couple of such incidents that occurred in his life.

Sir Cuthbert was captured at the Raid of Redeswire in 1575. This raid was a border skirmish between England and Scotland on 7th July 1575 and took place at Carter Bar, the Cheviot pass which enters Redesdale. Some of those involved beside Cuthbert were, on the English side, Sir George Heron and Sir John Forster, and I mention these two as you will see further on in this book that they are connected to the Collingwoods.

George Heron and his brother John were killed at Redeswire, and a number of others were taken prisoner, including Cuthbert. The Scots also carried out an impromptu raid on the local farms, taking around 300 cattle. The prisoners were held at Dalkeith Palace, the home of James Douglas, 4th Earl of Morton. James was the Regent for King James VI. Eventually due to various royal politics the prisoners were released with gifts and an apology for being held.

The story of the skirmish was turned into a border ballad, and in this ballad Cuthbert is referred to as "that courteous knight". On the Cheviot Hills near where the battle was fought, a commemoration stone was built. The stone reads "On this ridge, July 7th 1575 was fought one of the last border raids, known as The Raid of Redeswire". The battle is also commemorated annually by the Jethart Callant's Festival in July.

Another incident involving Cuthbert was that he was in a feud with William Selby of Twizell. In November 1586 on a journey home from Newcastle with his wife and daughter they met William, son of John Selby. Cuthbert was shot but survived but a companion, William Clavering, was killed. Another point of interest here is that the Heron family sold the Twizell estate to the Selby's around 1520's.

During my research I found the following children for Cuthbert and Dorothy, but I am not totally convinced that this is all of them. I think it is likely there were probably a couple of other children who died young and for whom the records are not very good. However, I will list the ones that I have found.

Dorothy	1561
Sir Thomas	1563
Anne	1563
John	1564
Jane	1566
Cuthbert	1567 (Lord Admiral Collingwood's line)
Robert	1569
Katherine	1570
Sir George	1571 (my line)
Rebecca	1573
Trevelian	1576

Notable information regarding these children

Sir Thomas 1563 married Anne Grey of Chillingham Castle. They went on to have three children, Mary 1590, Sir Robert 1592 and John 1594.

Sir Robert 1592 married Margaret Delaval. Sir Robert was Governor of Holy Island. Sir Robert and Margaret had a son named Daniel 1634. Daniel succeeded his father as Governor of Holy Island and Keeper of the Castle of Lindisfarne. Daniel was also an MP. Daniel is buried in Westminster Abbey in London, but in an unknown location. (There is more about Daniel in the Famous Collingwoods chapter).

SIR JOHN COLLINGWOOD 1512

Sir John, my great grandfather x13. Sir John was High Sheriff of Northumberland in 1544. Sir John married Ursula Buckton.

SIR ROBERT COLLINGWOOD 1486

Sir Robert Collingwood 1486 of Eslington married Lady Margaret Heron of Ford Castle. Sir Robert was High Sheriff of Northumberland. Sir Robert was included in a list in 1509 as a resident of Eslington able to bring 20 horsemen into the field. In the border wars he was involved in many raids. In 1520 he was rewarded for his part in the destruction of Scottish fortresses. Sir Robert commanded a garrison of 20 men at Eslington.

Sir Robert became a knight of the shire in the Parliament of 1529. The following year he was appointed as keeper of Wark, a border fortress second in importance to Berwick-upon-Tweed. Sir Robert took an active part in the dissolution of the smaller monasteries in Northumberland, and was one of those engaged in the task of seizing Hexham Priory. In February 1537 Sir Robert was advising the 3rd Duke of Norfolk about lawless elements in Redesdale and Tynedale, and later he was involved in the attempt to bridle them. Sir Robert and John Horsley corresponded with Cromwell on border matters and the Duke of Norfolk. It is reported that the Duke of Norfolk said that he trusted Collingwood above all others in that region. The Duke of Norfolk twice stayed at Eslington Park. Sir Robert was appointed Sheriff shortly after the rebellion, and again six years later, and this shows the confidence that was placed in him. He was described as "a wise borderer" and "a true man well minded to justice". Sir Robert also advised the Earl of Hertford and other commanders following the deterioration in relations with Scotland.

In February 1551 the Privy Council commanded Sir Robert and others to be conformate and obedient to orders from the deputy wardens of the East and Middle Marches. In April 1553 he paid £766 for a grant to himself and his brother Alexander of ex-monastic property in Northumberland, and he laid the basis of his estates in the county in 1542 when he bought the Eslington estate from Bertram Haselrigge.

Shortly before his death, Sir Robert distributed numerous annuities to his friends and relatives, some of which went to his grandson Cuthbert 1538. He invoked the intercession of the Virgin Mary and set up a chantry in Whittingham church. His descendants were to be recusants. Sir Robert also left a large annuity of £4 to a priest named Richard Lancaster.

East Lodge, Eslington Park

JOHN COLLINGWOOD ESQ 1455

John Collingwood of Eslington married Elizabeth Heron. My great grandparents x15.

SIR JOHN COLLANWOOD 1416

Sir John married Alicia Heselrige. It is here that we start to see the change in the way Collingwood is spelt.

WILLIAM DE COLLEINWOOD 1385

My great grandfather x17.

SIR ROBERT DE COLLINGEWOOD 1350 – 1425

My great grandfather x18.

Due to how far back in time we now are, I have not, as yet, found out any information for William 1385 and Sir Robert 1350.

Other possible ancestors....

The last two names I have found are Sir Robert Collingwood 1320 and Sir John Robert De Collingwood 1290, but I have as yet to validate this information. Being so far back in time it is not so easy. However, they would be my 19th and 20th great grandfathers if the information I currently have is correct.

CHAPTER FOUR

THE BORDER REIVERS

The Border Reivers were raiders in the lands extending either side of the English and Scottish border from the late 13th century to the beginning of the 17th century. The reivers were both English and Scottish. As England and Scotland were very often at war during the late Middle Ages, the livelihood of the inhabitants in that area was devastated by the various armies. People sought security through group strength and cunning, and they would attempt to improve their situation at the expense of their enemies.

Due to the rules of inheritance of land, following a father's death on the English side of the border in the 16th century it was sometimes the situation that the inheriting sons would not have enough land to enable them to survive, and this again was another cause of the reiver raids.

The English and Scottish governments alternated in their attitudes and went from indulgence, sometimes encouragement as the families served as a first line of defence along the border, to punishment when they thought the families had become too lawless. It is estimated that in 1584 the population of the English Middle Marches was approximately 120,000.

Border horses were small and lively and were trained to cross the difficult hilly and boggy terrain. It was easy for mounted reivers who knew the area well to rustle cattle, and they could cover many miles in a day. As time went on the original shepherd's plaid was replaced with light armour, and they had metal helmets, which is where the nickname "Steel Bonnets" comes from. They also carried various arms such as longbows, light lances, shields and light crossbows. As time moved forward they also would carry pistols, swords and dirks, (a dirk is a small knife).

The border reivers were sometimes in demand as mercenary soldiers as their skills as light cavalry were recognised. Some reivers fought in important battles such as Flodden Field 1513. However, the border reivers sometimes proved difficult to control when in the larger national armies. They would sometimes rob fellow soldiers in the camps. The reivers were more loyal to their clans than to the nations. During the battle of Ancrum Moor in Scotland in 1545, the reivers changed sides halfway through the battle to gain favour with the likely victors.

The families that lived in the border areas were on constant alert because of the raids and for this reason they built fortified tower houses. Quite often this was a two storey building and the family would go to the upper floor which was only accessed by an external ladder which would be pulled up when the family felt threatened. The walls of these buildings could be up to three feet thick and would only have narrow arrow slits for light and ventilation. This type of house could not be set on fire which gave the family some security as the attacking raiders would not want to spend time trying to get the family out. Another similar building was called a Pele tower, built for the same purposes but these were usually three stories high and were usually built for people such as heads of clans. The towers would often have an outer stone wall where cattle and livestock could be kept overnight.

March Law or Border Law developed in the region. This law entitled a person who had been raided the right to mount a counter raid within six days, including across the border, to recover his possessions. The rules stated that this "hot trod", (the lawful pursuit of reivers), had to proceed with hound, horn, hue and cry, and to make a racket and to carry a piece of burning turf on a spear to openly announce their purpose and to distinguish themselves from unlawful raiders. They might also use a sleuth hound to follow the raiders' tracks.

Both sides of the border were divided into Marches and each March had a March Warden. The duties of the March Warden included the organising of the patrols, watches and garrisons to deter raiding from the other side of the border. The Wardens also had the duty of maintaining justice and equity where possible. The Wardens from both side of the border would meet at agreed times along the border to settle claims against people their side of the border by people from the other side of it. These meetings were known as "Days of Truce" and were much like fairs with socialising and entertainment. For the reivers it provided an opportunity to lawfully meet with relatives and friends who were normally separated by the border. However, it was not unusual for violence to break out even on these days of truce. The Wardens were not that effective in maintaining the law. The Scottish Wardens were quite often border reivers themselves and complicit in raiding.

THE BORDER REIVERS

By the beginning of the 1600's things had got so bad along the border that the Government even considered rebuilding Hadrian's Wall! James VI of Scotland, (who became James I of England), took a stand against the reivers. He abolished border law and the term "borders" in favour of the term "Middleshires", and he dealt out stern justice to the reivers.

There are various songs and poems about the reivers. Hawick in Scotland holds an annual reivers' festival. Some of the Collingwoods and associated families were March Wardens.

One note regarding spoils in the English Middle March from Sir Cuthbert Collingwood 1538 to Sir Francis Walsingham, dated 23rd August 1587, states that on the 28th July 1587 twenty of East Teviotdale came in the evening to Eslington, Cuthbert Collingwood's dwelling house, and hurt two of his servants and took three geldings.

This is an example of what was happening on a very regular basis, and just during July and August of that year some 100 horses, 1,148 oxen and cows, 1,020 sheep were stolen in the raids and many men were hurt. Twenty prisoners were ransomed.

The Burn family were particularly known for their violence, and it is said that they killed seventeen Collingwoods in revenge for the killing of one of their own men.

Raiding was more predominant in autumn to spring, the time of year when crops and food were less readily available.

Border reivers at Gilnockie Tower, from an original drawing by G. Cattermole

CHAPTER FIVE

THE PELE TOWERS

Pele towers are found in Cumbria, Northumberland and the Scottish Borders. The towers are miniature castles built during the times of the raids by the Border Reivers. There are records of around 100 towers between 1500 and 1625, but there were probably many more. A lot of the towers were incorporated into houses at a later date, and some were improved and incorporated into castles.

Thomas Collingwood built a tower at Great Ryle in the 1500's. Thomas lost the tower in 1549 when it was taken over for mercenaries. In 1587 it was attacked by Armstrong of Liddesdale during a daytime raid. Nothing now remains of this tower.

When Thomas Clennel died his estate and Lilburn Tower went to his nephew Henry Collingwood 1757, who was High Sheriff of Northumberland in 1793. The estate was subsequently bequeathed to his son Henry John William Collingwood 1802 in 1820. In 1829 Henry Collingwood began construction of an Elizabethan style mansion. A foundation stone was laid and a time capsule of various items was placed under the stone. The items included various coins of the time, a newspaper and various vessels sealed with the arms of the Collingwood family. In 1842 after the death of Henry John William Collingwood the estate was sold to Edward John Collingwood 1815 of Eglingham, nephew of Admiral Lord Collingwood.

Hethpool House, Kirknewton, once the family seat of Admiral Lord Collingwood, which was built in the 17th century, has a 14th century tower, which is now an ancient monument and grade ll listed.

The Collingwoods were connected to various other Pele towers in Northumberland over the years.

CHAPTER SIX

THE JACOBITES

Following the 1715 uprising, the trials of those Jacobites who were captured continued during 1716. Twenty one men received a death sentence but only four were executed.

In July 1717 an Act of Grace was passed to pardon all those who had taken part in the 1715 uprising and who were still in prison. Another 33 were released in the north, the last of the Jacobite prisoners.

The Jacobites that had escaped were not pardoned but the authorities were not interested in pursuing these men. Some Jacobites had started new lives abroad. Several more lost their estates. Over 650 Jacobites were transported and some of these were Northumbrians, and they were given a seven year sentence.

Apart from the Jacobite George Collingwood as previously mentioned, another famous Jacobite was William Maxwell, 5th Earl of Nithsdale. Like George Collingwood, Lord Nithsdale was captured at the battle of Preston in 1715 and he was then taken to London for trial and was imprisoned in the Tower of London. He was found guilty of treason and was sentenced to death.

Grace Evans cottage

Lord Nithsdale was married to Lady Winifred Herbert, daughter of the Duke of Powis of Powis Castle, Welshpool, Wales. Upon hearing of his capture, Lady Winifred travelled to London from Scotland, an arduous journey due to heavy snow, and appealed for a pardon, but this was not forthcoming. Lady Winifred hatched an escape plan and the day before the execution was due to be carried out, she went to the Tower of London. With the help of a couple of other Jacobite supporters and her maid, Grace Evans, they carried out her plan which entailed Lord Nithsdale dressing as a woman and making his escape. He fled to Rome and his wife joined him there.

As a thank you to the maid Grace Evans, Lord Nithsdale gave her a cottage, which still stands today in Welshpool, at the bottom of Red Bank by St Mary's Church, and is known as "Grace Evans cottage". The cottage is now Grade II listed and is a private dwelling.

CHAPTER SEVEN

COLLINGWOOD SETTLERS

Over the years members of the Collingwood family have spread around the world, some of their own free will and some having no choice being convicts that were transported. It is from these family members that most of the current Collingwoods abroad descend from.

Some of the Collingwoods who migrated to America

Francis Collingwood 1780 from Rutland, Francis died in New York in 1849. Francis married an American and had eight children.

Charles Collingwood 1783 from Rutland, (brother of Francis), - arrived in New York in 1812 aged 29. Charles married an American and went on to have 16 children.

Francis and Charles are from my branch of the family, and my *Ancestry* results do show lots of cousins abroad.

Some Collingwoods who went to Australia

John Collingwood. John was a British convict who was shipped to Australia for life aboard the *David Clarke* for having forged notes. He arrived in Tasmania in 1841, (originally called Van Diemen's Land).

George Collingwood 1804. George was a British convict who was shipped to Australia for life aboard the *Earl St Vincent* in 1826, arriving in Tasmania.

Ann Collingwood, a British convict shipped to Australia for 14 years aboard the *Providence*. Ann arrived in Tasmania in 1825.

Settlers also went to New Zealand. By 1838 the British New Zealand Company had started to buy land from the Maori tribes and selling it on to settlers, and after the Treaty of Waitangi in 1840 many British families set out on the perilous six month journey to start a new life. One such family was **William Collingwood** 1844. William was originally from Lincolnshire where he lived with his wife and five children. The couple went on to have a further three children once they had arrived in New Zealand. From the records it looks like they settled in New Plymouth, New Zealand. William died in 1922 in New Plymouth.

CHAPTER EIGHT

THE CONNECTED FAMILIES

THE BOWES FAMILY

The first connected family I am going to write about is the Bowes family, which comes in when Lady Dorothy Bowes married Sir Cuthbert Collingwood 1538. Lady Dorothy Bowes is my great grandmother x12. It is through this link that the royal connections come in. Firstly through the Bowes family, who later changed the name to Bowes-Lyon, The Queen Mother, who is a cousin to myself and all the other Collingwoods who connect to this part of the tree, and likewise all descendants from the Queen Mother to the present day royals are all cousins.

Lady Dorothy's father was Sir George Bowes 1517, and his father and mother were Sir Ralph Bowes 1494 and Elizabeth Clifford. Sir Ralph 1494 was High Sheriff of Durham. Sir Ralph's parents were Sir Ralph Bowes 1468 and Margery Conyers. It is two of Ralph and Margery's sons that are of particular interest, Ralph 1494 as mentioned and Richard Bowes 1468, his descendants lead to the Queen Mother.

Sir Ralph Bowes and Margery Conyers are the great grandparents x15 that I share with the Queen Mother.

The Collingwoods

Sir Ralph Bowes 1468 married Margery Conyers

- Richard Bowes Esq 1488 *married* Elizabeth Aske
  - Queen Mother's line
- John Bowes About 1490
- Sir Ralph Bowes 1494 *married* Elizabeth Clifford
  - Sir George Bowes 1571 *married* Muriel Wycliffe
    - Lady Dorothy Bowes *married* Sir Cuthbert Collingwood 1538
- Sir Robert Bowes 1496
- ?

The Bowes family had been prominent in County Durham with their ownership of the estate and castle of Streatlam, but in 1713 Sir William Bowes 1656 acquired from his wife's family the Gibside estate, which included some of the area's richest coal seams and this led to the family becoming very wealthy through the coal trade.

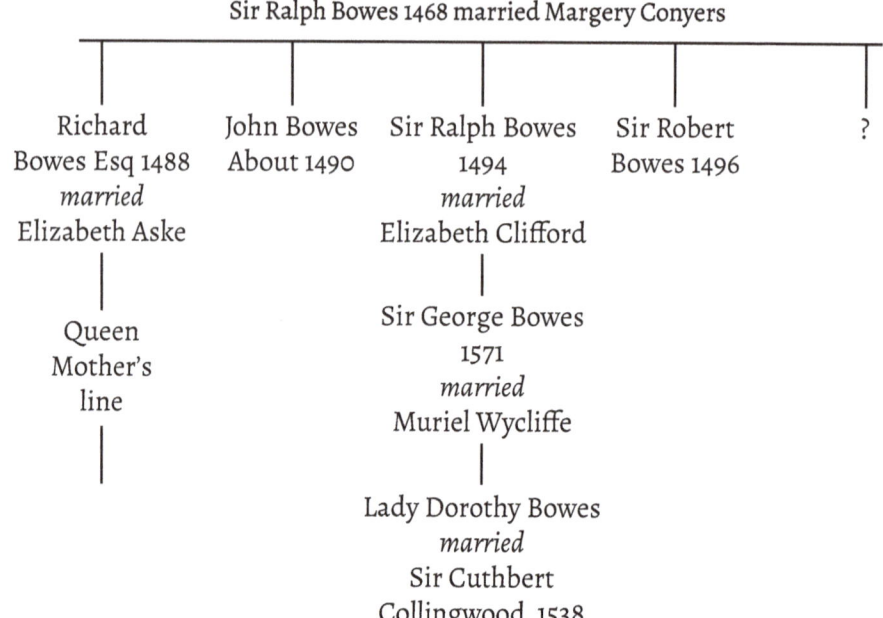

Gibside

Sir George Bowes 1701 was an English coal proprietor and Whig politician who sat in the House of Commons for 33 years from 1727 to 1760. He was the youngest son of Sir William Bowes MP and Elizabeth Bowes.

In 1767 Mary Eleanor Bowes married John Lyon, 9th Earl of Strathmore and Kinghorne, of Glamis Castle, Scotland. Mary was said to be the richest heiress in Europe at that time, and it was one of the conditions of marriage for her husband that he had to change his name to Bowes, and it is from this marriage that we get the Bowes-Lyons name, and even on one occasion Lyons-Bowes.

The main residences of the Bowes family were Gibside in Northumberland and Glamis Castle in Scotland.

Gibside is now a ruin and held by the National Trust. Glamis Castle is open to the public.

THE CLIFFORD FAMILY

As you will see from the Bowes tree, Sir Ralph Bowes 1494 married Elizabeth Clifford. This discovery of the Clifford family being in my family tree makes for very interesting reading, and came about via Susan Collingwood-Cameron. I came across some information about Susan whilst doing family research in Northumberland, and it turns out Susan is a cousin to me, and is quite closely related to Admiral Lord Collingwood as her great grandfather x2 was his brother. On a subsequent visit to Northumberland I managed to meet up with Susan and she was kind enough to share some more information on the family tree that she had.

Once I had the link to the Clifford family I have been able to trace the line back to King Edward III. As you will see from the tree on the next page, this makes very interesting reading.

King Edward III 1312-1371
married
Phillipa of Hainault - (daughter of William Earl of Hainault)
|
Lionel Plantagenet 1338-1368
married
Elizabeth De Burgh
|
Lady Phillipa Plantagenet 5th Countess of Ulster 1355-1378
married
Edmund Mortimer 3rd Earl of March 1351-1381
|
Elizabeth Mortimer 1371-1417
married
Sir Henry Percy (Hotspur) 1364-1403
(killed at the Battle of Shrewsbury - buried in York Minster)
|
Elizabeth Percy
married
John Lord Clifford 7th Baron 1389-1422
|
Thomas Lord Clifford 8th Baron 1414-1455
(killed in the Wars of the Roses Battle of St Albans
buried in St Albans Cathedral)
married
Joan Dacre – (daughter of Lord Dacre)
|
John Lord Clifford 9th Baron 1435-1461
(killed in the Wars of the Roses)
married
Margaret Bromflete
|
Henry Lord Clifford 10th Baron 1454-1523
married
Anne St John
|
Elizabeth Clifford
married
Sir Ralph Bowes 1494-1516

By my calculations this makes King Edward III my great grandfather x22. For those of you who watch the BBC's *Who Do You Think You Are* programme, you will probably recall the episode featuring Danny Dyer. Having looked at his tree that was researched by the BBC I can see that he also comes in on the Clifford family, (but not on the same Clifford as my line), and King Edward III is also his great grandfather x22!

Having now gained this link to the royal line I have been able to go even further back which I detail later on in this book.

THE DELAVAL FAMILY

The Delaval family is linked to the Collingwoods by the marriage of Sir Robert Collingwood 1592 to Margaret Delaval. The main Delaval estate was the manor of Seaton Delaval. The 18th century Delavals are known for their colourful lifestyle and for the magnificent Seaton Delaval Hall. They are also known for the development of Seaton Sluice and a coal mine at Old Hartley. The hall was destroyed by fire and the remains are now managed by the National Trust.

The Delaval name derives from Laval, a town in France. An early ancestor, Guy de la Val I, built a castle there in the first half of the eleventh century. Following the Norman conquest of England the de la Vals settled in Northumberland. At Seaton they built a small fortified dwelling near the existing Saxon church, which in 1100 Hubert de la Val rebuilt, bringing into being the present Church of Our Lady near Delaval Hall.

It would appear that the initial fortified dwelling evolved into the mediaeval Seaton Tower, probably in the fourteenth century. This was extended in Tudor and Jacobean times to form a rambling manor house of considerable size. In the earlier eighteenth century, this was replaced by the present Seaton Delaval Hall (always referred to locally as Delaval Hall), the third and last great mansion designed by architect and playwright Sir John Vanbrugh. This was devastated by a fire in 1822 but later restored, apart from the interior of the main block.

The Delaval surname died out on at least two occasions in the Middle Ages, but was re-adopted by the lords of Seaton

Seaton Delaval Hall with the author admiring the view.

presumably because of the prestige attached to its Norman-French sound. The Delaval family played a prominent part in the life of the county of Northumberland, several served as High Sheriff of the county, others became Members of Parliament and some served as Border Commissioner.

The fortunes of the Delavals of Seaton rose to their peak in the eighteenth century. However, with the death of Edward Hussey Delaval in 1814, the Delaval line died out, and the manor of Seaton Delaval and other estates passed to the Astley family of Melton Constable.

Edward Astley, 22nd Baron Hastings, a considerable landowner, spent many years restoring the Hall before it became his permanent home until his death in 2007. His son and heir, Delaval Astley 23rd Baron Hastings, faced with high death duties sold the Hall to the National Trust.

THE FENWICK FAMILY

Again linked by marriage, the ancient family of Fenwick had its seat from the 12th century at Fenwick Tower, Matfen, Northumberland, and from the 16th century at Wallington Hall. In 1378 John Fenwick was granted a licence to crenelate the house. The tower was largely demolished in about 1775, at which time a hoard of medieval gold coins was found. The remains of the tower are now incorporated into a 17th century farmhouse which has Grade II protection.

In 2010 human remains were found buried next to a cottage in the hamlet of Fenwick Towers, and radio-carbon dating of these remains indicated that they probably dated back to the 13th or 14th centuries.

Wallington is a country house and gardens about 12 miles from Morpeth. Wallington house is now under the National Trust after being donated by Sir Charles Philip Trevelyan in 1942, the first donation of its kind. The donation included the estate and farms.

The Fenwick Baronetcy was created in 1628 for Sir John Fenwick of Wallington Hall. Sir John sat as a member of parliament of Northumberland. The title became extinct when the third Baronet was executed for treason on 27 January 1697.

THE GREY FAMILY

The Grey family of Chillingham Castle is connected to the Collingwoods by the marriage of Sir Thomas Collingwood 1563, (son of Cuthbert 1538 and Lady Dorothy Bowes), to Anne Grey 1565. Chillingham Castle is now famous for being the most haunted castle in England. It is said that there is a link from Anne Grey to Lady Jane Grey but I have not got that far in my research as yet. However, it seems that Lady Jane Grey was a distant relation to the Collingwoods through the Lady Dorothy Bowes connection. The link to the Greys continues through the years and includes Lord Earl Grey of the tea fame!

Apart from being linked to Earl Grey tea, Lord Earl Grey was Prime Minister from 1830-1834. He was a member of the Whig party. Lord Earl Grey was a leader in multiple reform movements, and it was his government that enacted the Slavery Abolition Act 1833, bringing about the abolition of slavery in most of the British Empire. Lord Earl Grey is commemorated by the Grey's monument in the centre of Newcastle. The monument is a statue of Lord Earl Grey standing on top of a 130 foot high column.

Chillingham Castle is now owned by the Wakefield family and is open to the public. Chillingham is also linked to the wild cattle of Chillingham.

Chillingham Castle

THE HAGGERSTON FAMILY

Elizabeth Collingwood 1481, daughter of John Collanwood 1416 and Alicia Heselrige, married Thomas Haggerston of Haggerston Castle, Northumberland. The reason for mentioning this connection is that Haggerston Castle passed through several different owners after the Haggerstons, one of which was the Naylor family who lived at Leighton Hall, near Welshpool in Powys. Christopher John Naylor moved to live at Haggerston Castle after he inherited it and changed his name to Leyland after his benefactor. Christopher was responsible for the leylandii tree, and so, unfortunately, goes down in history as someone who has caused numerous neighbourly disputes over this fast growing tree.

Today the Haggerston Castle site is a Haven Holiday park and nothing really remains of the original Haggeston Castle, but there are some remnants of buildings on the site that were built in more recent times. However, in the remaining section of walled garden there is a wall plaque to commemorate the leylandii story.

THE HERON FAMILY

The Heron family owned Ford castle. The name Heron comes from Heron near Rouen in Normandy, and it is thought that Tihel de Heron was a Norman who came to England with William the Conqueror in 1066, and is found on the Battle Abbey Roll. Tihel was granted lands in Essex and his descendants spread to Northumberland, Hertfordshire, Scotland and Ireland.

Walter Heron was the clerk to William the Lion. William Heron was the keeper of Bamburgh Castle in 1248, the keeper of Scarborough Castle in 1255 and the Sheriff of Northumberland between 1246 and 1247. Chipchase Castle in the English Middle March was held by the Heron family for almost 300 years. The Herons also owned Ford Castle in Northumberland.

In 1300 Gerald Heron fought on the side of Robert the Bruce, and he was awarded lands of Kirroughtree where a branch of the family resided for 400 years. The family was in possession of Kirroughtree until 1889 when John Heron-Maxwell sold Kirroughtree to Major Arthur Armitage.

A border lord, Sir Gerard Heron put one thousand men in the saddle to attack William Wallace after he captured Kinclaven Castle. Roger Heron was a charter witness in 1321 in Langton, Berwick. Many Herons were transported to the Ulster Plantation during James's "pacification" of the Borders, along with many other border families.

Elizabeth Heron married John Collingwood Esq 1455. Sir Robert Collingwood 1486, High Sheriff of Northumberland, married Lady Margaret Heron.

Ford Castle is now owned by the Joicey family.

The castle is not open to the public but is an adventure and educational site for schools. However, visitors can visit the church, now an eco-museum site. Ford Village itself has a few areas to look round, including Lady Waterford Hall.

Ford Castle

THE LIDDELL FAMILY

As previously mentioned in this book the Liddell family are distantly related to the Collingwoods. The Liddell family, apart from now owning Eslington Park, also own Ravensworth Castle in Northumberland.

The Liddell family descends from Thomas Liddell, a wealthy merchant of Newcastle-upon-Tyne and supporter of Charles I. In 1642 he was created a Baronet of Ravensworth Castle. His grandson, the third Baronet, represented Durham and Newcastle-upon-Tyne in the House of Commons. In 1720 he acquired the estate of Eslington Park. His grandson, the fourth Baronet, sat as Member of Parliament for Morpeth and in 1747 he was created Baron Ravensworth of Ravensworth Castle.

The main seat for the family was originally at Ravensworth Castle. This great stately home was almost completely demolished in the 1920's due to subsidence, ironically caused by the family's own coal mines beneath, the profits of which had paid for its construction. The castle's stables, which survive in a ruinous state, were featured in the BBC's *Restoration* television programme in 2003.

CHAPTER NINE

FURTHER BACK IN TIME

Continuing back in time from King Edward III, the family tree continues back through the Plantagenets and all the way back to 846 where I have found Rollo the Viking.

Rollo 846-931
married
Poppa of Bayeux
(both buried in Notre Dame Cathedral Rouen)
|
William Longsword 893-942
married
Sprota
(both buried in Notre Dame Cathedral Rouen)
|
Richard l (The Fearless) Duke of Normandy Count of Rouen 932-966
married
Emma of France
|
Richard ll (The Good) Duke of Normandy 966-1026
married
Judith de Rennes
|
Robert l (The Magnificent) Duke of Normandy 1000-1035
|

King William l (The Conqueror) Duke of Normandy 1028-1087
married
Matilda of Flanders 1030-1083
|
King Henry l of England Duke of Normandy 1068-1135
married
Matilda of Scotland 1079-1118
|
Geoffrey V Plantagenet Count of Anjou 1113-1151
married
Empress Matilda 1102-1167
|
King Henry ll 1133-1189
married
Eleanor Duchess of Aquitaine 1122-1204
|
King John 1166-1216
married
Isabelle of Talliefer Countess of Angouléme 1188-1246
|
King Henry lll 1207-1273
married
Eleanor of Provence 1217-1291
|
King Edward l (Longshanks) 1239-1307
married
Eleanor 1244-1290
(both buried in Westminster Abbey)
|
King Edward ll 1284-1327
married
Isabella Princess of France 1292-1358
|
King Edward lll

Rollo the Viking would be my great grandfather x35. Rollo would appear to be a nickname and it is said that his real name was Hrolf Ganger. Rollo was born in the mid 9th century, it is believed in Norway. It is said that he is descended from noble lineage. The earliest mention that I have found of Rollo so far is of him leading Vikings who besieged Paris in 885-886 but were beaten back by Odo of France.

During one of Rollo's raids, the King of West Francia offered him lands between the mouth of the Seine and what is now Rouen in return for Rollo ceasing his raiding. Rollo accepted this offer and this made him the first ruler of the lands which would become Normandy and his people would become Normans.

Rollo's descendants became the Dukes of Normandy with William the Conqueror coming to England and becoming King.

A statue of Rollo stands in the city of Rouen.

Rollo became a Christian and took the baptismal name Robert.

This find in my tree is extremely fascinating and will lead to a lot more research.

Rollo of Normandy, Rouen ©

CHAPTER TEN

FAMOUS COLLINGWOODS

There are many famous/well known Collingwoods apart from Admiral Lord Collingwood and I will list some of those that I have come across....

Major Daniel Collingwood 1634-1681

Daniel, (who I have previously mentioned in this book), was an English politician, Member of Parliament for Morpeth 1679-1681. Daniel was educated at Warkworth and Cambridge. He had a commission in a troop of guards. He succeeded his father to become Governor of Holy Island and was appointed Keeper of Lindisfarne Castle.

Daniel was asked to build a fort on Holy Island, (known as Osborne Fort or Steel End Fort). The fort is also referred to as "the fort on the Heugh". Constructed in 1671, the fort is now a ruin and is on the opposite side of the harbour from the castle. The purpose of the fort was to supplement the defences already offered to Lindisfarne's harbour by the artillery mounted on Lindisfarne Castle.

Lindisfarne Castle, Holy Island, Northumberland, drawing, Thomas Girtin 1796

The remains of this fort are scheduled under the Ancient Monuments and Archaeological Areas Act 1979 as amended as it is regarded by the Secretary of State to be of national importance. Another interesting connection with the fort is that it has been discovered that there is an underlying midden beneath it. The midden was discovered following coastal erosion and is considered an important archaeological site. Evidence discovered suggests that the Heugh has been occupied at various times for the past 8,000 years. The erosion damage has been repaired but further archaeological remains await discovery in the future.

Roger Collingwood 1495-1517

Roger was an English mathematician, elected a fellow of Queens College, Cambridge. He was Dean of his college and in 1507 obtained a license to travel on the continent for the purpose of studying canon law.

Jane Collingwood 1740

Whose line comes down from Sir Robert Collingwood 1486, married Admiral William Dickson and they had …

Sir Archibald Collingwood Dickson 1772

2nd Baronet. Archibald was involved in the battle of the Glorious 1st of June 1794, the siege of the Dutch fleet in 1799 at Vlieter and the Battle of Copenhagen April 1801.

and …

... Major General Sir Alexander Dickson 1777

Fought in the Napoleonic wars and the Peninsular war of 1812. Sir Alexander Dickson's son was General Sir Collingwood Dickson 1817 who was awarded the Victoria Cross for his part in the siege of Sebastopol. He received the award on 26th June 1857 from Queen Victoria in Hyde Park, London.

If you are interested in this particular branch of the family there is a lot more information available in books and on the internet about all the siblings and descendants.

William Pole Collingwood 1829

The third son of Henry John William Collingwood 1757 and Frances Emily Carnaby Haggerston of Cornhill House, Northumberland. William 1829 was in the army and was in active service in the rebellion in Ceylon in 1847. He became a Lieutenant in the 21st Regiment in November 1851 and then became Captain in July 1854 where he witnessed active service in the Crimea. William was present at the siege and capture of Sebastopol and the capture of Kinburn. He was onboard the steamer ship the *Spartan* which was wrecked off Dog Rocks on the coast of Africa in July 1856. It was on this occasion that he was senior officer of the troops onboard and he won a mention in General Orders.

William was given the rank of Major in April 1867 and continued to advance through the ranks. He eventually became a Colonel and was in the Zulu wars in 1879. After he retired from command he was subsequently appointed the new command of the Fifth Regimental District, Newcastle-upon-Tyne.

**William Gershom Collingwood
1854-1932**

English artist and archaeologist.

**Robin George Collingwood
1889-1943**

English philosopher.

**Sir Edward Foyle Collingwood
1900-1970**

English mathematician and scientist.

**Peter Trevor Collingwood
1920-2016**

English born Australian actor.

FAMOUS COLLINGWOODS

Lyn Collingwood 1936
Australian actress famous for being in Home and away.

Charles Collingwood 1917-1985
American television newscaster

Charles Henry Collingwood 1943
British Actor. Charles has featured in various productions including the long running radio show *The Archers*.

Paul Collingwood 1976
English cricketer.

Parliamentary Harquebusier Officer c1645
© Chris Collingwood

Chris Collingwood

The final person I would like to mention here is the historical artist Chris Collingwood.

Although not as famous as some of the other Collingwoods, I came across his website during the course of my research and was amazed by the quality of his artwork, especially as he specialises in historical scenes.

You can check out his excellent repertoire of paintings and drawings on his website:

www.collingwoodhistoricart.com

CHAPTER ELEVEN

MISCELLANEOUS

For those that are researching their family tree, the history of Admiral Lord Collingwood or the Battle of Trafalgar there are numerous publications on these subjects.

The Trafalgar Way map was shown to me by my cousin Susan Collingwood-Cameron and I managed to find my own copy on ebay for a few pounds. The map shows the route that the messenger, Lieutenant John Richards Lapenotiere, took to deliver the news of the naval victory and the death of Nelson to the Admiralty in London. The map also contains other historical information.

Another very useful tool that I came across is the Collingwood Ancestry website, which has been created by Gordon Collingwood. Gordon has spent, well I don't know how many hours but certainly a lot, compiling a database of 99 branches of the Collingwood family. It is an excellent website and free to use once you have signed up. Not only is it a big help in researching Collingwood family trees, there is a lot of other useful information on there as well. www.collingwoodancestry.com

Gordon is also keen for Collingwood males to consider taking a Y-DNA test with FamilyTreeDNA.org and join the Collingwood DNA Project. The 'Y' chromosome is passed from father to son down the paternal line just like the surname. It rarely mutates with each successive generation and Gordon discovered his great grandfather x6, John Collingwood who was born in 1661, by matching with a man who was born in South Africa. Such is the power of this DNA test that two living people today have the identical Y-DNA as an ancestor born so far back in time. Gordon gives more information about this on his website.

Newbiggin-by-the-Sea has a Family History Centre where they are endeavouring to list the family history of the whole town. They already have a database of more than 35,000 people who have lived in the town and are happy to assist people who are doing family tree research. There are a few Collingwood records in this database.

Before going to print, I discovered more connections regarding the Herbert family of Pembrokeshire and Powis Castle, Welshpool.

The Collingwoods are connected to the Percy family of Northumberland through Lady Dorothy Bowes, and the Percys are linked to the Herbert family through marriage. One of the marriages was between Maud Herbert and Sir Henry Percy, 4th Earl of Northumberland.
A descendant of Maud and Sir Henry was Winifred, wife of Lord Nithsdale, as mentioned in the Jacobite chapter.

An interesting final point on Maud's line is that two generations forward, William Herbert married Anne Parr, sister of Catherine Parr, Queen of England, Henry VIII's sixth wife. George Herbert, 5th Earl of Carnarvon, of Tutankhamun fame, is a descendant of William Herbert and Anne Parr.
The family seat for this branch of the family is Highclere Castle. Today Highclere Castle is very well known as it was the filming location for the extremely popular TV series Downton Abbey.

There could also be further connections to the Herbert family via the Clifford and Grey families, but this will need further research.

Highclere Castle

www.ingramcontent.com/pod-product-compliance
Lightning Source LLC
Chambersburg PA
CBHW041958080526
44588CB00021B/2797